Introductio

This is my fourth book on cake decorating and I don't think I have shown you how to make a rose yet; there are still so many delightful animal and human figures that can be fashioned from icing and used to create unusual birthday or special occasion cakes. When you say "I'll bring the cake" and they expect roses, then, you show up with a queen on a throne, an enchanting nature scene or a totally unexpected mother pig and litter — it does create a "stir."

And these figures are so easy to make; it is not necessary to be an artist — the proper combination of icing and pressure will create the most dramatic *dimensional* figure more quickly than it can be sketched with a pencil — depth and perspective come instantly out of the tube, rather than being slowly shaded in.

Technical accuracy is a matter of personal knowledge or research; however, 90% accuracy will give you 100% effect — just get the bulk of the figure right and don't fret over little details if they are not perfect. And feel free to take "artistic license" when working with frosting — eyes can be moved to *glare* to the front or a mouth full of teeth may be exaggerated — cakes are for immediate pleasure, not for posterity.

Once you have perfected a figure, see how often you can use it (by simple change of size or position) to fit a cake of your own design: a bear can become a team "Bruin" or Santa's small ram may be transformed into "Aries".

All the cakes in this book may be made with either buttercream or boiled icing. If made correctly, the upright figures will travel just as well as those piped flat. A good example is the Hunter With Camera cake — created for our son-in-law, Alan, and piped in buttercream, this birthday cake was transported two hundred miles and arrived in perfect condition.

Because of my commercial background, I normally refer to rectangular cake sizes as one-fourth, one-half, or full sheet cakes; however, the non-commercial decorator may think of cake pans in terms of inches: ½ sheet = approximately 12"x16", ¼ sheet = approximately 8"x12" or 9"x12".

When piping figures, I believe better results are obtained by using a parchment paper cone, as its lightness gives much better feel and control of pressure — and *pressure control* is the key to success in figure piping. Also, when using a parchment cone, try cutting the end off to form a small or medium point or press the point flat and cut it into a small leaf tube; the same cone of icing may often be cut two or three times, providing a variety of sizes and shapes in a minimum amount of time. However, for larger size openings, like a #10 round, always use a metal tube.

An artist's palette knife is a most useful tool for smoothing and shaping figures and iced pieces of cake. They have light, flexible blades and come in a variety of shapes and sizes.

When practicing figures before making a cake, work in an area the size of the cake pan you plan to use or you will be inclined to make the figures too large for your cake.

A slightly different technique is used in figure piping to achieve a smooth and natural look. Many times, a part of a figure (such as a shoulder or rump) is blown out from "inside"— the tube is inserted into the figure and held there, and a gentle squeezing of the bag causes the icing to swell (build up) into the desired shape, without a "stuck-on" look.

All the cakes shown in this book were made in our kitchen at home (using a household size mixer) and taste-tested by Rascal (our white cat) who ate the nose off the witch. So why not step into your own kitchen, whip up a batch of fluffy delight and see how much fun figure piping can be.

Frog Pond

This ¼ sheet cake, iced in pale green, is a busy, busy cake — with its little pond, fallen tree, many rocks, cattails, and water loving friends.

The pond is a smear of blue piping jelly — any shape you desire. The log is a tapered strip of extra cake or a strip cut from the end of your sheet cake. (Round off the top of strip.) To ice the log, use a medium cut point (#7) and load the bag with two shades of brown icing; ice both ends first using the tube and a circular motion (medium pressure). For bark, draw a line starting at large end of log and extending slightly past small end; for roots, insert tube at large end and pull out tapering lines. Rocks are made using a medium cut point (#7) — streak bag lightly with brown, tan, pale yellow, and gray icing; fill with white icing — squeeze out a number of irregular-shaped mounds. (Note: Do not streak bag with food color as rocks will be too brilliant.) For cattails, use a medium cut round (#7) and dark brown icing; insert a broom type straw into bag (about one-half

inch) and squeeze gently while pulling straw out of bag — insert straw into cake. Curly vines and bushes are made with a fine cut point (#3). For vines, use heavy pressure and pull tube along, creating the curly effect; for bushes, use heavy pressure, but remain in one spot — lift tube slightly as bush builds up. Swamp grass is made with a medium cut leaf (#67), green and yellow icing; pull leaves straight up and let ends bend over. SWAN/DUCK/-GOOSE . . . Use a medium cut point (#7) and white icing; pipe a heavy shell for the body, pulling towards you and tapering gently upward to finish in a pointed tail. Add a small shell on each side for the wings. Neck and head are made in one continuous action — facing front of body, insert tube (at water) and with very light pressure squeeze out neck; continue up front of body — pushing neck back over top of body — lift tube, and come forward and slightly downward, to finish with the head. Head may be folded down on the neck or lifted high in the air depending on the consistency of your

icing. (See small picture of yellow swan.) Swans make a very attractive small cake all by themselves, and in the world of cake decorating — why not "yellow", "pink" or "blue" swans. The bill is a tiny leaf cut (#65), pulled out in two short lines. Two black piping jelly dots form the eyes. **HALF-DUCK** . . . Half-a-duck fills up space and adds variety. Hold tube (medium cut point (#7) straight up and down; start squeezing (heavy pressure) — lift tube — and with lessening pressure continue upward — flipping the tail forward. For upper legs, insert tube and gently pull out two, short, white lines. With a fine cut point (#3), orange icing, come downward (from upper legs) to the water; add a fan of three short lines for the webbed feet. **BABY DUCK** . . . Use a fine cut point (#3), yellow icing — pipe a small shell, pulling end upward for tail; add a tiny ball for the head. If you wish wings to show, pull two little "flips" out from the sides. Add black dots for eyes and use a tiny cut point #2, in orange, for the bill.

FROGS . . . Using a fine cut point (#3) and dark brownish-green icing, pipe a heavy, tapering line — slanting forward and upward. With same number tube (yellow) support the body by adding a chest (piped upward). Insert the tube (fine cut point (#3), brownish green icing) into rear of body, and pipe a "V" shaped leg on each side of body. Insert tube at top of body and pull front leg down, and out, hiding seam where yellow and green meet. Repeat on other side of body. For head, add a small tapering ball. With brownish-green icing and very fine cut point (#1), add a fan at the end of each leg for the webbed feet. Use same tube for features on head, adding two small balls on top where the eyes will be. Insert tube and blow out both cheeks, then, draw a double connecting line between them. A tiny dot of yellow icing for the eyes (over-piped with yellow piping jelly), and a tiny, vertical line of black for each pupil complete the frog. Frogs may be made in assorted sizes, or pipe "heads only" sticking out of the water. Frog splashing in water uses same tubes as other frogs; the body is a long, tapering shell — front legs are pulled forward, and rear legs pulled backwards in a bent position. Add feet.

For splashed water around duck— make half-a-duck first, then, pipe a white icing ring around him (in the piping jelly water) and tease it upward with the point of a palette knife. For the leaping frog, the splashing water must be added before piping the frog.

Grrrow! Don't Go Near The Water! *Bayou Cake*

This ½ sheet cake features a scene from deep in one of our Southern swamps and is ideal for a hunter or nature lover. To enhance the "out-doors" feeling, the traditional, rectangular cake-shape has been altered — by rounding off the corners and digging out some of the sides. If desired, these cut out pieces may be added to the cake sides to increase the rustic ffect. Ice in a light green, with cut out areas done in light brown. The pond is blue piping jelly with a little brown piping jelly smeared over it for the muddy look. The swamp grass, rocks, bushes, fallen log, and splashing water are the same as those on the Frog Pond cake. (Note: Many things used on one cake may be successfully incorporated into another; learn to "steal" from yourself — when you have mastered something on one cake, try to use it, whenever you can, on others.) The animals, shown here, are easily made and blend together nicely to create a scene, or each may

be used as a central theme for a cake of his own.

LITTLE BEAR IN TREE . . .
Use a flex-straw for the tree; bend straw at flexible joint to form the branch. Spiral-wrap the plastic straw with masking tape if using buttercream. Use a medium cut point (#7) loaded half-and-half with a light gray and a tan icing; with medium pressure, pipe icing up and down straw to form tree; pull out roots and cover branch. For body of cub, use a medium cut point (#7), black icing; with tapering pres-sure, pipe a shell upward (on tree) — stopping in a blunt end. Add small ball for head — slide down — and (light pressure) pull out nose (middle of ball). Insert tube at shoulder and (light pressure) pull out short line for front paw. Repeat for other front paw. For hind leg, insert tube at bottom of shell, blow out a slight haunch (light pressure), and come out of body for leg; change direction with tube and add a tiny paw. Pipe other hind leg

in same manner, but have leg going upward — as if bear is climbing tree. With a fine cut point (#3), make two loops on the head for ears; use same tube for accent lines over eyes. The eyes are small dots of yellow piping jelly with black piping jelly centers. A black, heart-shaped piping jelly nose is added. With same size tube and white icing, add claws. **CROCO-DILE/ALLIGATOR . . .** This fierce appearing creature is much easier to make than it looks. Use a (#104) rose tube (wide edge up) and greenish-brown icing; with heavy pressure, pipe a straight line for the length of the body, then, continue on (with tapering pressure) to form the curved tail. (One line = one body and tail.) For front leg, insert medium cut point (#7) half way up body (at shoulder), and with light pressure, come straight out (short line), then straight down to water. Repeat on opposite side for other front leg. Move to rear, and (just before tail) repeat procedure for hind legs. Using tube #89 (held at low angle — light pressure) start at front of body and with very slight "bouncing" motion, travel length of body, fading into tail; repeat for total of three rows (side by side). With a fine cut point (#3), light yellow icing, mark off length of lower jaw (using back-and-forth motion) — go from body, outward, to end of lower jaw. Hold flat, wood, coffee-stirrer-stick (4½" long x ⅜" wide) in one hand, cover about three inches of one side (back-and-forth motion) with yellow icing; insert stick into lower jaw at start of body — upward angle, icing side down. With tube used for legs, outline lower jaw (light pressure). Starting at front of body, on top of stick, pipe (heavy pressure) a heart-shape for head, and continue (heavy pressure) up length of stick for the upper jaw. With light pressure, outline sides of stick to conceal it. Insert tube, and blow up two balls (light pressure) on top of head, where eyes will be. With fine cut point (#3), pull out short "fanned" lines, at end of each leg, for feet. Insert same tube at end of snout and pipe two light circles, upward, for nostrils — overpipe if necessary; open nostrils with blunt end of toothpick. Flesh-colored tongue is made with fine cut point (#3), light pressure. Use fine cut point (#2), white icing, (light pressure) to pull out many, many teeth, and add claws. With fine points of piping jelly, apply the eyes: first yellow, then red, topped with a black streak. **BEAR** . . . The bear is made on a paper, disposable, wedding cake pillar (7¼" length x ¾" diameter) or four straws, wrapped together with masking tape, may also be used. Insert paper tube about two inches into cake; using a medium cut point (#8), black icing (heavy pressure), start at back of tube — about one inch from bottom — and run a heavy line to top of tube. Repeat on both sides, and front. Insert decorating tube at bottom of side line — blow out heavy haunch — reduce pressure — bring short leg forward and down. Add short, forward line for paw. Repeat on other side. Insert tube into side (at shoulder) and (medium pressure) pull front leg out. Repeat on opposite side. Front legs should hug body, as much as possible, to provide support. Close any gaps or seams, in body, using point of decorating tube and light pressure. For head, make heavy line across top of paper tube; if necessary, overpipe (towards front) for forehead. Drop

down to middle of head, use light pressure, and pull out nose. Using a fine cut point (#3), black icing (light pressure and strokes), tease out fur all over bear (except on face and muzzle). Pipe two, little, looped lines on top of head for ears. Add arch lines over eyes and continue down to form top of nose. With medium pressure, pull out short line, under muzzle, for lower jaw and tease fur around it. With light pressure, pull out longer fur on sides of head. Using a fine point of yellow piping jelly, pipe two eyes; add black dot of piping jelly for each pupil. With black piping jelly, pipe heart-shaped nose and continue down and around open mouth. Tiny leaf cut point (#65), in pink, is used for tongue. For teeth and claws, use fine cut point (#2), white. Where paper tube shows (between bottom legs in front and back) pull up grass with leaf cut point (#65), green icing, or bear may be leaned against log, as shown in side view. Leaning the bear against log hides the front of legs and provides additional support.

Some Decisions in Life are Painful...

BEAR ON CACTUS CAKE

This is a cake with a "message" . . . for that "hard to express" special occasion.

Use a small (6 inch) round cake, adding a piece of cake on top to build up the contour. Rough ice in a light desert tan, streaked with a darker brown. Cacti are made with a #199 star tube pulled upward around the sides of the cake. (Note: If desired, a tiny flower may be added, at top, to conceal bump where tube was lifted off of cactus.) Form the main cactus (on top) by inserting a straw well into the cake, then pushing the tube, and bag of green icing, down over the straw, to the cake top; with very light pressure, pull bag upward to end of straw. Placing candy rocks on the cake adds to the decoration and (if needed) provides support for the small cacti. The little brown bear, at top of cactus, is made the same way as the one in the Bayou cake, Page 4.

SKUNK . . . Use a fine cut point (#3) and black icing; with heavy pressure, make a line across the bottom of the tall cactus for body of the skunk. Pull a heavy line upward (on cactus) for the tail. With medium pressure, pull four, very short lines downward from the body to the cake top, for the legs. Add a small ball at end of body for the head; reduce pressure, drop down, and pull out the tiny nose. With very light pressure, form two loops for ears, then, tease the tail outward for a furry effect; tease the body downward for a furry effect. Insert a fine cut point (#2), white icing, into end of tail and pipe a "skunk" stripe extending from tail to nose. Small dots of black piping jelly are used for the nose and eyes.

HUNTER WITH CAMERA CAKE

The modern day hunter — armed with a camera not a rifle — stalks his prize trophy, not as yet aware that mother bear is there.

The bear, log, and rocks — in this outdoor scene — are borrowed from cakes already shown (Bayou & Frog Pond); the only change is in the colors. The ¼ sheet cake is iced in green, streaked with tan. The sides are trimmed with a leaf cut (#67) in dark green, pulled upward (bouncing motion) to make the fern-like bushes. The upright green tree is described on page 18. **HUNTER** . . . The body of our intent photographer is made using two, medium cut point (#7) tubes: one orange, one blue. Notice the body is built up off of the cake in an inverted "V" shape; the legs support the shirt and also support each other. With the

orange tube (medium pressure) start at the cake and pull shirt upward and towards you, stopping in a blunt end. The blue pants are an inverted "U" shape; start on cake (medium pressure) go upward and forward to shirt, form a slight ball — slide over — form another slight ball and come down to finish on cake. Insert orange tube into shoulders and pull out sleeves. Scoop out hole where neck will go; pipe a ring around hole, for collar, and to help support head. Use medium cut point (#5), flesh color, for legs and arms. For legs, start at bottom of pants, pull out a tapering line — increasing pressure at calf and decreasing at the ankle — add a short line for the foot. Toes are made with a fine cut point (#2). For arms, start at the sleeves, pull tapering lines forward and together (leaving space for

the camera). Pipe in camera and pull fingers over it; use short, curved lines — starting with the little finger and building to thumb (fine cut point, (#2). Use your blue tube to add fringe at bottom of pants. Head is same as for Queen, page 25, except a beard and mustache are added and hair is shorter. **CUB BEAR** . . . Use medium cut point (#7), brown icing. With tapering pressure, pipe a blunt shell on the ground. In one continuous movement — add a round ball for the head — shut off pressure — slide down — and squeeze out a little nose. Insert tube at shoulder and pull out a short line for the front leg (on ground). At heavy end of shell, pull out a short line (light pressure) for the hind leg (on ground). Add a tiny paw. With a fine cut point (#3), white, (light pressure) insert tube into body at front leg and pull a stripe down "tummy" to rear leg. Add two top legs in same manner as legs on ground, but note they stick out into the air. With a very fine cut point (#2), brown icing, add two loops on top of head for ears. A tiny line for the lower jaw may be pulled out under the nose if you wish mouth to be open. Using very fine points of black piping jelly, pink icing, and white icing, add eyes, nose, tongue, teeth and claws. **CAMERA** . . . The camera, camera case, and gadget bag are basically rectangular blocks of icing trimmed with fine points. The camera lens is three circles of white icing filled with piping jelly.

A Cowboy and his Horse...

THREE, HORSE CAKES

A new and unusual way to make a very versatile horse (in any size) has been used on the three (12"x16") ½ sheet cakes shown here. The horse has been piped in small, medium, and large sizes — the largest one measuring fourteen inches from nose to outstretched hind hoof. This method is the easiest and quickest way to form a "very large" horse with a minimum amount of piping pressure and extra work — only a soft, flowing icing is required. For smaller horses, the basic tube to use is a #5; for large horses, move up to a #10 as the basic tube.

The smaller the horse the more background or "filler" needed, as shown in the Cowboy Roping Steer cake. In addition to the sky and rough ground area (used on all the cakes) more elaborate details have been added to this one: White icing clouds streak the sky (#3 tube); tan bluffs rise up in the background with tree studded, rolling, green hills at their base. With light brown icing, outline the bluffs — fill in — and stroke downward with a palette knife. Dark green hills are outlined, filled in, and stroked sideways with palette knife. Trees may be made using a small leaf

cut tube #65 (pull out branches) or with a #16 star tube bounced upward for bushy effect. Make bushes using a fine cut point (#3). The small cowboy and horse figures, on this cake, are balanced by the running steer. The steer may be made in the same manner as the horse shown here or like the cow on page 19.

For the Old Cowboy cake, a medium size horse figure is used (#10 round tube) requiring less background filler. This tired old horse differs from the others in head, neck, and leg positions: the head and neck are drooped, and the legs are brought down in a standing position. Drooping eyelids and ears, frazzled mane and tail show his youthful days are long past. The ladder is made with a medium cut point (#5); it may be added before or after making the old cowboy, but be sure his boot rests on one of the rungs. Cacti are pulled upward with a medium star tube. The spider web is made with an extra fine cut point (#1) — pipe a spoked wheel effect and connect the spokes with short lines.

The cake with the largest horse and rider uses these figures to cover its entire top — as the horse is 14" long, there is neither room nor need for additional filler. Use a star tube (#18) to pipe the top border; for an interesting variation, try using a large basket tube (#47st, teeth side up) for a weathered barn-wood look or the same tube (smooth side up) for a stretched-rawhide frame.

HEAD 'EM OFF AT THE PASS.. AGAIN --!!

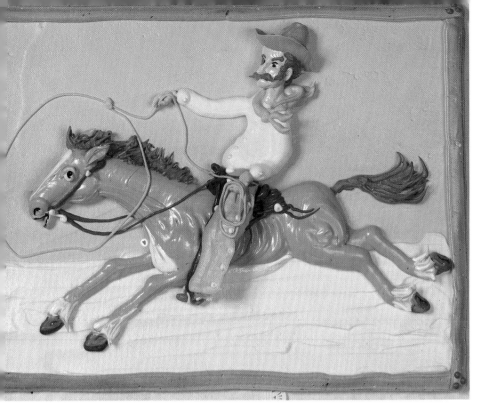

A Very Large Horse

LARGE HORSE . . . Use a large round tube (#10), gray icing, medium pressure — pipe one, long line to form top of neck, back, rump, and (decreasing pressure) one hind leg. The neck area slants downward; the back is slightly swayed (more so if comic effect is desired); the rump rises upward; the hind leg goes back, then down, with a little upward flip at the end. The body is one continuous roll (heavy pressure) that finishes in a curved line for bottom of neck; begin roll at rump and work toward front of horse. The lines of the roll must **not** be distinct, they should blend together, and on the upward part — scoop into, and fuse with the body line. (Note: Roll forming the body will be easier to make if cake is turned so that neck faces you.) For front leg on far side of horse, insert tube into edge of body—come forward (light pressure) —pause to form joint, and continue downward in a slanting line. For second front leg, insert tube at shoulder –- blow out slightly — drop down, and come forward to joint, pause, and continue downward in slanting line. To make top, rear leg, insert tube at rump — use heavy pressure — circle and build up rump; with decreasing pressure come downward and backward to joint, then continue down leg, finishing in a slight backward flip. On end of neck, pipe a heavy, tapering shell for the head. With a medium cut point (#7) — pull out two ears — add an arched line over each eye — add a flared line around nostril area (to shape nose). Insert tube into "head" shell (under eye) and blow out a heavy swell for jaw line; reduce pressure and slide downward along shell, then, increase pressure slightly and pull out a short line forming bottom of open mouth. With blunt end of a toothpick, scoop out hole in nostril and slit in ear. Using a medium cut point (#5), black icing, pull out short, flowing lines for mane and tail and add a heavy check-mark to form each hoof. Use a medium cut point (#5), white icing, and blend a heavy line into chest and "belly" areas; add a blaze down front of head; pull out short, feathered lines over hooves, and pipe a large dot for protruding eyeball. With a fine cut point (black piping jelly) outline open mouth, add pupil to eye, and pipe a little black into nostril. With small palette knife, smooth off seam on neck and on rump build-up, if necessary.

SADDLE: . . . With a medium cut point (#7), brown icing, pipe a rectangular outline over back, and down side of horse — fill in and smooth off. With heavy pressure, add a downward-tapering line to front of rectangle for pommel; add saddle horn to top of pommel. Draw a curved line upward (light pressure) at rear of rectangle for cantle. Pipe a heavy, curved line downward from bottom of rectangle and add a yellow loop for stirrup. The reins and additional saddle trim are made with fine points of brown icing and white icing. (Note: If a cowboy is riding the horse pipe him on first, then, pipe on only the parts of saddle that will show.)

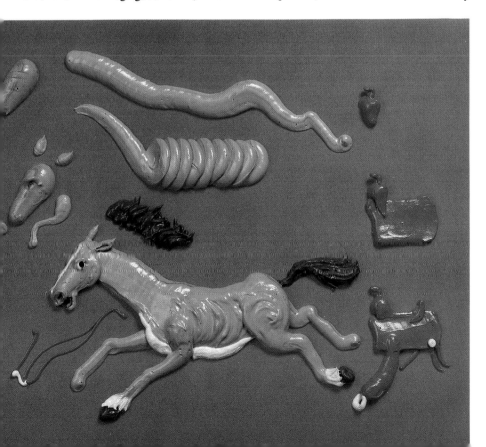

The Cowboy

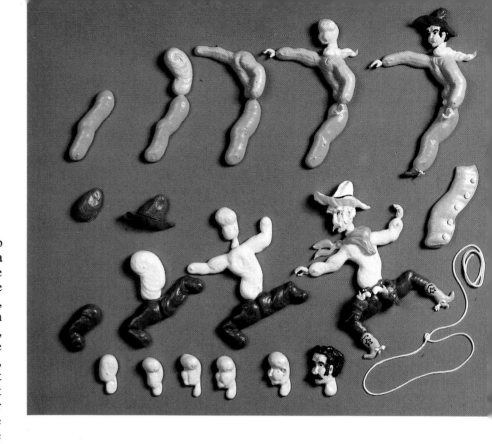

RIDING COWBOY . . . A cowboy, to fit the large horse, is made with a medium cut point (#7) and blue icing. As the cowboy is sitting in the saddle, and has only one leg showing, start the leg above the saddle — a medium heavy line, piped downward, with a slight bend at the knee for the pant leg. If you wish to add chaps, use a #127 rose tube — lay it flat on top of the leg (wide part to front of leg) and follow the leg contour downward. The colored shirt is made with a medium cut point (#7); angle the tube against top of pants and pull shirt upward (medium pressure) stopping at the shoulders. For a heavier stomach, exert more pressure at start of shirt. The arms are added by inserting tube at each shoulder and pulling a line outward (light pressure) to end of sleeve — the throwing arm is piped directly onto the top of the cake — the holding arm is piped on top of the body for greater buildup. Try for a natural look by bending arms, slightly, at elbows. Pipe neck and head upward from shirt, then add neckerchief around and trailing from neck using a medium cut point (#5). The hands are made with a fine cut point (#3); pipe a small ball against end of sleeve — pull out the little finger, then stack other fingers or top of it — add the thumb last. The throwing hand is made somewhat open; the holding hand is curved. With a fine cut point (#3), yellow icing, coil the loops of rope in holding hand, then continue up through throwing hand and out to the end of loop. **HAT** . . . With a medium cut point (#5), pull a tapering line upward from head for crown of hat. Add brim using a #104 rose tube (wide part against crown); start on cake (on one side of crown) — go across crown — and finish on cake on the other side. Creases or indentations in crown may be made with the blunt end of a toothpick. **BOOT** . . . Use a fine

cut point (#3), start at bottom of chap, and (light pressure) pull a tapering line forward for front of boot; add high heel and pipe stirrup around boot. Spurs, buttons and silver ornaments are made with a fine point of white. **OLD COWBOY** . . . Use a medium cut point (#7) and black icing; start on cake (above horse and ladder), and with slight pressure, pipe a ball forming half of rump — continue downward and forward — bend at knee, and finish with a very short line, stopping where boot top will begin. Pipe a second ball against the first one and pull leg upward — bend at knee, and finish in a short line. **SHIRT** . . . Use a medium cut point (#7), gold icing, and medium pressure—pull shirt upward (curved line) to shoulders; insert tube at shoulders and (light pressure) pull arms out to ends of sleeves, bending at elbows as shown. Add hands, neck, head, hat and neckerchief. **HOLSTERS & GUNS** . . . Using dark brown icing, a fine cut point (#3), and light pressure — add crossed gun belts; with heavier pressure add tapering lines for holsters. With a fine cut point (#3), gray icing, pipe a small section of "gun" rising out of holsters; finish off with a curved white line for pearl handles. **BOOTS** . . . Use a fine cut point (#3), and, with heavy pres-

sure, come downward from pant leg for top part of boot — change direction — use light pressure and continue to toe of boot; add high heel. Repeat for second boot. Spurs and design on boots are made with very fine points of black icing. **SIDE VIEW HEAD** . . . The same oval shape is used for both side and front view heads — the difference is in the placement; in a side view, the oval is set to the left or right side of the neck, depending on the direction the figure will be looking. With a medium cut point (#5), light pressure, pipe a short line upward for neck; increase pressure and pipe an oval upward for head — placing it slightly to left side on neck. Insert tube on side of oval and blow out forehead, piping upward. Drop down, insert tube at cheek (nearest cake) — blow out cheek (light pressure) — and fade downward to chin. Insert tube and blow out top cheek — slide downward and add chin. With very light pressure, insert tube into forehead — pull straight line downward between cheeks, for nose, ending in a slight loop. Add a curved line for the ear. With a fine cut point (#2), add hair in color of your choice. (Note: The hair is used to build out back of head) Add sideburns, mustache, and eyebrows in matching color. Use piping jelly for eyes. And remember— "good guys" wear white hats.

The Ghosties and Goblins are here...

HEADLESS HORSEMAN CAKE Amidst the whistle of the wind and shrill cries of the night creatures, comes the thunder of hooves and a piercing whinny—the Headless Horseman rides again!!!

This departure from the usual Halloween cake is a ½ sheet cake (12"x16"). The sky is iced in pale blue and streaked with a watered-down, purple, paste color; the rough-iced ground is light brown. The tree and corn shock frame horse and rider; however, the tree is more in the foreground and the corn shock in the background. **TREE** . . . Use a medium cut point (#7), streak the bag with

brown color and fill with brown icing. Make a series of (overlapping) up-and-down lines for the trunk (medium pressure). Insert tube at bottom of trunk and pull out tapering lines for the roots; insert tube at top of trunk and pull out long, tapering lines for branches. With point of tube, dig out three holes in trunk (for eyes and mouth) and lightly pipe an oval around each; insert tube between them and pull out a short, tapering, downward line for the nose. Fill in eyes and mouth with black piping jelly for a dramatic effect. **MOON** . . . For the full moon, pipe a circular outline onto the night sky, with a medium cut point

(#7) and bright yellow icing; fill in using a circular motion and smooth off with a small palette knife. (Note: For an exact, circular outline, you may "touch" the cake, first, with the rim of a glass or a round cutter; use the appropriate size.) **HORSE:** A good example of "borrowing" a decoration from one cake and using it for a totally different theme — instructions for the horse may be found in the cowboy section of this book. **TRIM** . . . Leaves are made with the cut leaf tube used for the corn shock. For border, use a #18 star tube (loaded half-and-half with orange and yellow) and a simple back-and-forth motion.

Hallowe'en Figures

HALF-PUMPKINS . . . Using a #10 round tube (orange icing) pipe two quotation-mark shapes (one to the right, one to the left) touching at top and bottom; use heavy pressure at top, fading out as you move downward. Pipe a set of *narrower,* quotation-shaped lines on top of the first pair. The hole in center is covered by piping a fifth line over it (top to bottom) exerting heaviest pressure in center section of line. (Notice all the pumpkin sections taper down and finish on the cake, this, combined with the heavy pressure used at the top, results in desired, slightly forward tilt.) A short, brown stem at top and a leaf or two at the bottom completes the pumpkin. JACK-O-LANTERN-FACE . . . With a fine point palette knife, dig out holes for the eyes and nose and a curved slash for the mouth; fill with yellow piping jelly. Add two, red piping jelly eyes, black piping jelly dots for pupils, a red icing tongue (small leaf cut tube), and white icing teeth (fine cut point). BATS . . . Use black icing and a fine cut point (#3), pipe a short, heavy, tapering line for the body. Outline the wings on each side (light pressure) and fill in, using light pressure and a back-and-forth motion. If piping a large bat, details may be added by pulling out a little pointed line for the head and two little pointed ears. The wing area may be smoothed off with a small palette knife. CORN SHOCK . . . Use a fine cut point (#3), brownish-yellowish-tan icing, and pipe an isosceles triangle (light pressure); fill in with up-and-down lines — do not let lines build up too thick at the top. With a fine leaf cut point (#65) and light pressure, pull leaves from top of triangle (upward) and bring the tips down. The small pumpkins, around base of corn shock, are made with a medium cut point

(#5) and orange icing — use same method as for large pumpkin.
OWL . . . Use a medium cut point (#7), medium brown icing, and pipe a heavy shell for body. Hold tube vertically and pipe two balls at top of shell for head; as each ball is finished, pull icing off to right or left to form horned ear tufts. With a fine cut point (#3), draw a wing-shaped line — outward and upward — from each side of body, for top of wing; add feathers underneath. (Note: As wing is open, start with a back-and-forth motion for upper part of feathers, gradually changing to an up-and-down motion nearer body.) Use a fine cut point (#3), yellow icing, and add two lines for eyes, pull out pointed beak and claws. Two fine lines of black piping jelly complete eyes. HEADLESS HORSEMAN BODY . . . Use a medium cut point (#7), white icing; with medium pressure, pipe body downward from shoulders to horse's back, then, forward to knee — change direction and finish in a tapering point. Insert tube at shoulders and draw out two arms: one straight forward, one bent at elbow and folded over. Give motion effect to sleeves and bottom of figure by inserting tube, and (fading pressure) pulling out short, flowing lines. Add Jack-O-Lantern head. WITCH ON BROOMSTICK . . . Size of witch is determined by size of moon. The smaller the witch, the smaller round point you will use. For the broom, pipe a slanted line and "feather" the end. Draw the stick figure as shown in picture. With heavy pressure, follow the stick figure downward from shoulders to bottom of robe — insert tube at shoulders and draw heavy sleeve forward to broom. Pull a tapering line upward from shoulders for head and pointed hat; cross base of hat with fine line for brim. With

light pressure, insert tube at back of head and pull out flowing hair (short lines); insert tube in bottom of skirt and pull out wider, flowing motion lines. Using light pressure, pull a line outward and downward for nose; pull out tiny "jutting" line for chin. With rolling motion, add fingers over broom. Add shoe at end of skirt. Finish with yellow eye — overpiped with red piping jelly. Note: Piping a very large Witch-on-a-Broomstick (covering the top of an eight inch cake, iced yellow) makes a simple, yet effective, Halloween party cake. RUNNING BLACK CAT . . . Use a medium cut point (#5), black icing, heavy pressure — pipe a slightly curved hot-dog shape; reduce to light pressure and pull out hind leg, as shown on instruction board. Insert tube into edge of body and pull out a straight line for front leg. For second front leg, insert tube into top of body— blow out shoulder — come down, then forward in a straight line. For second hind leg insert tube at rear of body, blow out haunch, and (fading pressure) pull out hind leg. Insert tube at front of body and pull out a short line (medium pressure) for neck, ending in a "ball" for head. Insert tube at rear of body and (light pressure) pull out tail. Add feet (fine cut point (#3) by making three, tight circles at end of each leg. Insert tube into middle-front of head ball and pull out a very slight nose, then, with point of tube, dig out the open mouth and pull out slight line for lower jaw. Pull out two, backward-slanting ears. With a fine point of black piping jelly, add nose and outline mouth. With very fine point of white icing, add claws and teeth. Eyes are slanted line of yellow icing with a red piping jelly dot for pupil. If desired, hair on back may be teased upward using a fine point of black icing.

"Bubble, Bubble Toil and Trouble . . .

WITCH CAKE

"A watched pot never boils" — except when a "wicked witch" is the watcher. This wicked witch is a perfect example of the dramatic effect upright decorations can create on a cake.

Use a ¼ sheet cake, in yellow — trim the top edge off two cup cakes and set one of these (top side down) in center of cake. **CAULDRON** . . . With medium cut point (#7), black icing, start at bottom of cup cake, and, by spinning the turntable, pipe a spiral of icing — around and upward — to top edge of cup cake. Smooth off and shape cauldron with a small palette knife. Hold tube vertically, and (medium pressure) pipe two rings around top for the rim. Fill pot with red piping jelly. With a fine. cut point (#2), white icing, pipe a bone or two into the pot. Streak a bag with brown color and fill with brown icing, then, using a medium cut point (#7), pull out short lines, around base of pot, for fire logs. Streak a leaf cut point (#65) with red piping jelly and fill with yellow icing; pull "dancing" flames (upward) around cauldron. Smoke is made with same tube as that used for bones in pot. Stain three, five-inch cotton swab sticks (swabs removed) with brown food color and insert into cake, forming a tripod over the cauldron. (Note: Broom straws or bamboo skewers, covered in brown icing, may also be used.) For skull, use a medium cut point (#5) and white icing; pipe a ball into top of tripod and pull a short line downward from ball for lower part of skull. Use same tube as for "smoke" and pipe a series of small bounces across lower skull line, for teeth. Use fine point of black piping jelly to fill in eye sockets and nose hole. **JACK-O-LANTERN** . . . Place second trimmed cup cake at top corner of cake (top side down). Use orange icing, a #10 round tube (held at a slight angle), and form the pumpkin — a series of vertical lines pulled upward; start each section at base of cup cake and (medium pressure) pull upward, increasing to heavy pressure — fade out fast — ending where the stem will be. With a fine point palette knife, dig out holes for the eyes and nose and a curved slash for the mouth — fill with yellow piping jelly. With red piping jelly, add two eyeballs and a "glow" to the nose. Black piping jelly is used for vertical pupil lines. Pull out tongue with tube used for "flames". Use "smoke" tube for teeth. **SMALL PUMPKINS** . . . To add small pumpkins on cake top, squeeze out three balls of icing, then, pipe the vertical sections (upward) around them. **LEAVES** . . . Use a leaf cut point (#67), streaked with autumn-colored icing, for leaves on bottom border and top of cake. **SIDE TRIM PUMP-KINS** . . . These pumpkins are made in same manner as those on the Headless Horseman cake, page 11. Use a #10 round tube (held horizontally), point tube at cake side and pipe pumpkins directly against side of cake. Add witch as shown in step-by-step pictures.

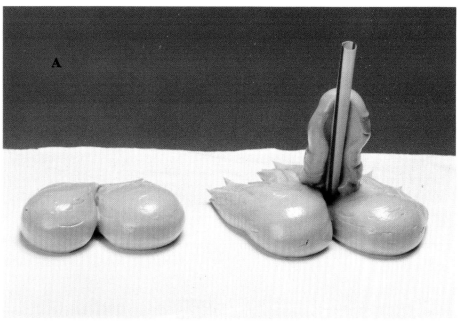

WITCH FIGURE . . . (A) — Upright witch is made with the aid of a plastic straw. If using buttercream icing, spiral-wrap the straw with masking tape. Use a #10 round tube and gray icing, hold tube vertically, and pipe two, heavy, connected shells. There will be a seam between them; insert straw (tilted slightly forward) into this seam at about the middle of the shells. Pipe a heavy line up back of straw. Insert tube into back of shells and (light pressure) pull out ragged edges on skirt.

WITCH FIGURE . . . (B) — Pipe a heavy line up front of straw — insert tube at shoulder (on side), use medium pressure, and draw a line downward to elbow –- change direction — pull line forward, over heavy, front part of shell, finishing in a blunt end with a downward flair. Repeat for other sleeve. (Note: Sleeves hide side seams of body and help support it, they should be piped tightly against body.) Create a ragged effect on front part of sleeves by inserting a medium cut point (#5) into sleeve and pulling downward (fading pressure). Scoop out ends of sleeves with a fine point palette knife. **HEAD** . . . Use a medium cut point (#7) and a most "unflattering" shade of icing for the complexion — a witches blend of gray, pink and yellow. Allow one inch of straw to extend above body, cut off any excess. Point tube directly at straw (where it joins body) — squeeze gently and lift tube slightly to form neck; pull tube slightly away from straw (increase pressure) and pipe an oval (upward) the remaining length of the straw. Let the icing roll over top of straw as shown. Ignore back of head, as it will be covered with hair. The angry, arched lines over eyes are tapered from the outside toward center of head. Drop down (leaving space for the eyes), insert tube at cheek and pull a *long*, tapering line, straight downward Repeat on other side and finish in a little ball for the chin. (Note: The face must be long to accommodate the large, open mouth. As the straw is tilted forward, pulling the cheeks downward will give the witch face a desired, forward-thrusting look.

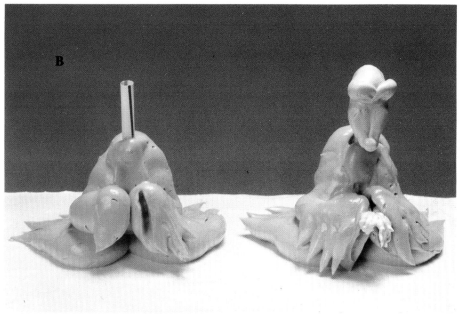

Witch Figure

WITCH FACE TRIM . . . Use a fine cut point (#3), same "witchy complexion" color, and add bags under eyes. Open the mouth with a fine point palette knife; above mouth, insert tube and pull outward and downward for nose. Finish off by adding a small wart on one side of nose. Fill in eyes with yellow piping jelly; use red piping jelly and a fine cut point to add eyeballs and an accent line under each eye. A very fine point of black piping jelly is used for vertical pupil. Insert tongue, in mouth, using a fine cut point and red icing. White icing and a fine cut point (#2) are used for the one tooth, the eyebrow, and the wild hair. With heavy pressure, build out back of head, then, with light pressure, tease hair outward and upward.

HANDS . . . With same tube used for face trim, pipe hands coming out of sleeves; start with a ball inside the sleeve opening; with very light pressure and a "shaky" motion, pull fingers out (one at a time) — start with little finger, work upward, and finish with thumb. Fingers may be curled and perhaps the forefinger pulled straight out in a "spellcasting" manner. The shaky motion will result in the characteristic gnarled, witch-like appearance of the hands.

"What'll you have... Light or Dark?"

A different approach to our Thanksgiving Bird graces this holiday cake . . . no fuss, no feathers . . . just slice and serve.

Use a ¼ sheet cake iced in pale green. The colorful leaves around the sides are made with a #352 leaf tube. Lightly streak a bag with orange and brown icing, and fill with a golden yellow; pipe a standard leaf shape using light pressure. With end of tube (no pressure) flick out tiny points on leaf edges. For color variation, turn (streaked) bag over and repeat procedure. Use a very, very tiny point (dark brown icing) and add the stems and veins. Add bottom border with a medium cut point (#8), brown icing. **GRAPES** . . . Use a small cut point (#3), purple icing, and pipe a heavy, pointed shell for the base. Start at the pointed end and cover the base with very tiny, overlapping shells — making sure **only** the rounded ends are showing. For a more "irregular" bunch, add a few "round ball" grapes over the shells. To make curly vines, hold a fine cut point (#2) one-fourth inch above grapes (slight angle, medium pressure) and move along in a straight line; the icing will curl itself. Add leaves, using a tiny leaf cut point (#65). **CORN** . . . Use a #133/233 tube and golden icing; hold tube at a very low angle, and with light pressure and a very slight up-and-down motion form the corn kernels. (Note: Too much up-and-down motion will result in a misshapen effect as shown in first ear of corn, line 3.) Length of corn may be doubled by adding green shucks with a leaf cut point (#65). **CARROTS** . . . Use a round cut point (#5), orange icing, and light pressure — pull out a "bunch" of tapering lines. For tops, use green icing and a round cut point (#2); draw a series of straight lines from the carrots — lift tube slightly, at end of each line, and apply heavy pressure to form curly tops. Parsley under turkey is made in same manner as carrot tops. **TURKEY** . . . The turkey is built over a wedge shaped piece of cake (rounded at top). With a medium cut point (#7) and brown icing, pipe a broad-breasted turkey-shaped ring of icing around base of cake wedge. Ice wedge (same tube) adding extra icing where the breast or sides need building out. Smooth off and shape body using a small palette knife. Insert tube into each side of breast (at bottom); use light pressure and pipe three continuous lines (forming a triangle) for the wings. Insert tube at bottom (rear) of bird; squeeze a short, heavy line forward and upward for the thigh; stop pressure, change direction, and (medium pressure) squeeze out the heavy part of the drumstick; continue tapering downward (reducing pressure) to end. Repeat for second drumstick. (Note: Be sure to cross drumsticks.) Thigh and drumstick can be piped in one continuous line or you may break it at the drumstick. A small triangle of icing under the crossed drumsticks forms the tail.

"Where's the Milk and Cookies?"

SANTA CLAUS IN ROCKER . . . CAKE

This ¼ sheet Christmas cake finds Santa pausing for a moment of rest — after placing toys, for the good girls and boys, beneath the gaily decorated tree.

The cake is iced in white and the large, oval shaped, green rug (covering most of the top) is made with a #18 star tube (slight back-and-forth motion). The pink christmas tree is made on the outside of a rolled parchment cone — like the green tree shown on page 18. For trim, use a very fine cut point (#1) and white icing; hold tube about one inch away from tree — squeeze (very heavy pressure) — and spiral popcorn around branches; using tweezers, add silver dragees to popcorn. Sprinkle finished tree with edible glitter for a "sparkling" effect. A white tree, sprinkled with colored, crystal sugar (as its only decoration) makes a very pretty variation. The bag full of "goodies" is made with a medium cut point (#7), tan icing; with heavy pressure, pipe a large, irregular ball— taper forward, and (light pressure) pipe a circular, hollow opening. Leave space between bag and tree for Santa. TOYS . . . Toys around sides of cake are made in assorted colors using a medium cut point (#5). The doll, teddy bear, and rabbit are all shells

with a little "ball" head; arms and legs are short lines pulled out from the shell. The bear has a tiny line pulled out for the nose, and loops for ears; the rabbit has tapering lines for ears and a tiny ball for a tail; the horse is really a heavy stick figure; the doll has a skirt made with a slight back-and-forth motion (light pressure) — shoes and curly hair are also added; the baseball glove is a ball of icing with fingers pulled out. Toys on top of cake are made the same way as toys on sides, but with a smaller tube — #3. Other simple toys, that might be used, are a clown, chicken, dog, duck or even a toy car outlined and filled in. Miniature candy canes, placed at each corner, provide an added Christmas touch. Instructions for making the royal icing Santa in Rocker figure are located below.

SANTA IN ROCKING CHAIR
STEP-BY-STEP BOARD

The ideal chair for Santa's rest is this 3¼ inch high (solid back) plastic rocker. Santa may be made ahead of time by using a hard drying royal icing — (make several at one time and keep the extras for future use). When piping a figure into a rocking chair, the chair will have a tendency to rock; to counteract this, either lay the chair on its back or prop something against it while piping the figure. Some recent, red food colors tend to break down royal icing, however, Holiday red shade was used here and proved very satisfactory in both color and keeping qualities.

(1)—Use a #7 round tube (medium pressure) and form the first leg by piping a ball on one side of chair seat; continue forward to front edge of seat — reduce pressure — bend line downward and finish (in a blunt end) midway down front of chair. (2)—Repeat for second leg. (3)—Starting at legs, pipe torso upward (heavy pressure) against back of chair. (Note: Do not cover entire back of chair — leave room for head.) With medium pressure, pipe line on top of and across legs, for skirt of coat. (4)—For arms, insert tube at each shoulder, pull short line downward (medium pressure), bend at elbow and continue line forward, resting on arm of chair. (5)—Use a #5 round tube, black icing, and add a line across body for belt. Boots are

easier to add if chair is on its back; with heavy pressure, pull a short line down, from end of each pant leg, for top of boot — change direction — with light pressure, pull toe upward. For head, use flesh colored icing and a #3 round tube; pipe a heavy oval shape (on top of torso) firmly against back of chair. In front, center, of oval — pipe a small ball for nose; beneath this, add two larger balls for cheeks. (6)—For hat, use a #7 round tube (red icing) and pipe a sideways-tapering line on top of head. Add fur trim to Santa's outfit with a #2 round tube (white icing) and a slight

"bouncing" motion. (Note: Be sure to add white trim line on each side of Santa where bottom of coat would be.) (7)—Use a #3 round tube, red, for mittens; pipe a short, heavy line outward from each sleeve, and (light pressure) add a thumb. With a #2 round tube (white icing) — light pressure — stroke the long hair and beard downward; add eyebrows and handlebar mustache. A ball of bright yellow icing is added for belt buckle and two "twinkling-blue" piping jelly eyes complete jolly old Santa Claus.

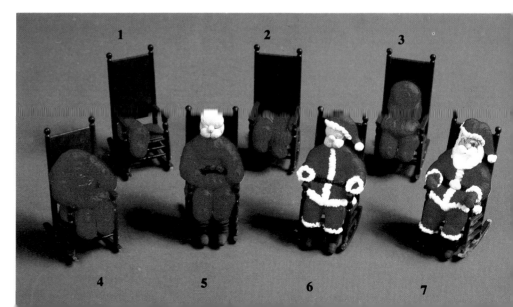

'Twas the night before Christmas and all through the house . . . came a great clattering sound — not tiny reindeer feet, but chimney bricks falling — as, with a mighty effort, Santa flew onward, shouting to his unusual team — on, Old Gray Mare! on, Little Piggy! on, Goosey-Goosey-Gander!

If you are tired of the standard Christmas cake, why not try this one— for the office party or to amuse and delight your family.

Ice a ½ sheet cake in pale blue. With a medium cut point (#7), outline, fill in , and smooth off two triangular shapes (one yellow, one tan) at bottom edge of cake top. Use any of the basket tubes, or even a small leaf, for shingled sections of roof; pipe one row at a time, starting at bottom. Outline, fill in, and smooth off chimneys; create brick effect with fine cut point of white icing; loose bricks, flying through air, are made with a #7 tube. Add snow on roofs with a medium cut point (#7), white icing, downward strokes. Pipe Santa and team according to directions; add a few loose feathers and with a fine cut point (black piping jelly) sketch in "motion" lines. The border is made with a #10 tube, white icing, using a figure-eight motion.

If a conventional type cake is desired, substitute the team of reindeer for the humorous animal team.

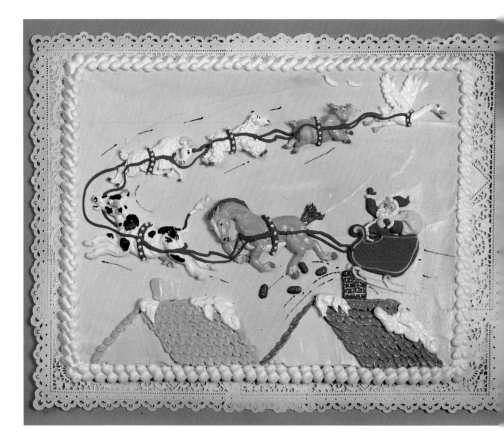

TREES . . . STEP-BY-STEP

The simplest and quickest way to make a tree is to use the material you have on hand; parchment paper and icing. The trees, shown here, were made by rolling a piece of rectangular parchment (9"x12") into a cone. Tape the cone together with masking tape and cut off the open end, so the tree will stand level. With a medium leaf cut point (#68), run green icing (roughly) up and down the parchment cone and smooth it off with a palette knife. Starting at bottom, pull leaves out — working your way up to the top. (Note: Be sure to pull leaves downward — then out — this will enable you to cover more space with fewer leaves.) Finished tree stands 7½ inches tall. For different size trees use different size cones.

Santa's Animals

The top three rows of animals, shown on the instruction board, read downward; the bottom two rows read across.

RAM . . . (1)—With a medium cut point (#7), medium pressure, pipe a short, curved line (to left) for neck — increase pressure — and continue with a heavy, straight line (to left) for body. (2)—Return to start of neck, and (medium pressure) pull a short, tapering line downward for head; add a slight (upward) flip of icing, at rear of body, for tail. Insert tube into edge of body and (light pressure) pull out front and hind leg—bending as shown. (3)—For second front leg, insert tube into body at shoulder — squeeze (medium pressure) to build up shoulder — come downward slightly, and (light pressure) continue forward and downward to finish leg. Insert tube into rear of body — build up rump (medium pressure) — with decreasing pressure continue downward, as shown, to complete second hind leg. Insert tube into side of head and lightly pull out one ear. Use a fine cut point (#3), yellow icing, and a slight "bouncing" motion to form curved horns. Use a very fine cut point (black piping jelly) for features on head, and a fine cut point (#2), black icing, to pipe two, tiny balls on the end of each leg for split hooves. Hairy effect on ram (on cake) is made by gently stroking the body (light pressure) with a very fine cut point (#1), white icing.

SHEEP . . . (1)—With the same tube (#7) of white icing, and heavy pressure, pipe a short, downward-slanting line (to left) for neck — increase pressure — continue with a heavy, straight line (to left) for body; add a little ball for tail. (2)—Return to start of neck and add a short, slanting line for

head. Insert tube into edge of body and (medium pressure) pull out straight lines for front and hind legs. (3)—For support, pipe the second pair of legs directly on top of the first pair; insert tube into body and (medium pressure) pull out each leg. Insert tube into head and lightly pull out one ear. For features and hooves, follow instructions given for Ram. Wooly effect on sheep (on cake) is made with a very fine cut point (#1) — white icing — bounced gently (light pressure) over the body area.

PIG . . . (1)—Use a medium cut point (#7), pink icing, and heavy pressure — pipe a short, plump, hot-dog-shape for body. (2)—Add a ball for head. Insert tube into edge of body and (light pressure) pull out a very short front and hind leg, as shown. (3)—Insert tube into front side of "head" ball and (medium pressure) pull out a short, blunt (upward) line for snout; finish it with a very thin line around upper edge; insert tube into ball and lightly blow out cheek. For second front leg, insert tube into body at shoulder — squeeze (medium pressure) to build out shoulder — decrease pressure and pull the very short leg forward and downward. For second hind leg, insert tube into rear of body and (medium pressure) build up the "ham" — decrease to light pressure and pull short leg back and down. Use a fine cut point (#2), pink icing, and add arched line over eye; insert tube at rear and pull out coiled tail. If using a paper point, press it flat, cut to a small leaf shape (#65), and pull out two, flying, pointed ears. With a fine point of white, pipe two small balls for eyes. Add pupils, nostrils, and

mouth line with a fine cut point of black piping jelly. Hooves are made as for the Ram.

GOOSEY-GOOSEY-GANDER . . . Body, neck and head are all one line. (1)—Use a medium cut point (#7) and white icing — begin piping at tail (light pressure) moving to right with increasing pressure (to build up body) — continue onward (decreasing pressure) for long arched neck — finishing in a small ball for head. With light pressure, draw a line upward (as shown) for leading edge of wing. (2)—With light pressure and a back-and-forth motion, start at body and add wing feathers. (Note: Feathers change direction the farther out the wing you go.) (3)—With very light pressure, pull out short, tapering lines for tail and upper portion of each leg. Using light pressure, pull leading edge of second wing upward from body; add feathers. Eye is a black dot of piping jelly. With a fine cut point (#2), orange icing, pull out short lines for lower portion of legs and add a tiny fan, at end of each, for webbed feet. With same orange tube, pull out two, short lines for open bill.

COW . . . Pipe a hot-dog shape for the body using a medium cut point (#8), white icing, and medium pressure. (2)—Insert tube at left end of body and (lighter pressure) pipe a short line (angled upward) for the neck; continue on, adding a tapering shell for the head. For legs, use a medium cut point (#7), white icing, and light pressure; insert tube at bottom edge of body (front and back) and pipe as shown. (3)—For second front

and hind leg, insert tube at shoulder and rump — build up shoulder and rump (medium pressure) and continue into leg (light pressure) forming each leg into stretched-out, running position, as shown. With light pressure, pull tail outward and upward from rump, feathering it (short lines) at the end. To enhance cow-like shape, make body deeper by insterting tube back of front leg and piping a stomach line under body. To add brisket and broaden neck, insert tube between front legs and pipe a small shell upward — fading out along neck. With a fine cut point (#3), white icing, add trim to head; broaden top of head by inserting tube on far side and piping a line (light pressure) across top of head (horns will be added at each end of this line) — beneath line, pull out a single ear; insert tube into side of head, under ear, and (light pressure) blow out forward-curving jaw line — continue downward to form open mouth; with light pressure, pipe one eyeball and add arched lines over each nostril and the eyeball. Use a fine point of black piping jelly for pupil and to outline nostril and the open mouth. Use a fine cut point (#3), yellow icing, to pull out horns. The split hooves are made with a fine cut point (#3) and brown icing. Udder is made with a fine cut point (#3) and pink icing — add a ball under body and pull out three faucets: one for regular, one for low-fat, and one for chocolate. If a spotted cow is desired, paint spots on with thinned-down paste color.

HORSE . . . With a medium cut point (#8), gray icing, heavy pressure, pipe the basic "hot-dog" shape. (2)—Insert tube at left end of hot-dog and (heavy tapering pressure) pull out arched line for neck; on end of neck, add tapering shell for head. With a medium cut point (#7) and gray icing — insert tube at front edge of body and (light pressure) pipe leg forward, down, and slightly back, as shown. Insert tube at rear end of body and pull hind leg backward, down, and slightly backward. With a fine cut point (#3), white (heavy pressure) pull a line under chest and tummy of horse. (3)—For second front leg, use the #7 tube and build out shoulder (medium pressure), continuing downward into leg (light pressure), and bending backward as shown. Insert tube into rump and blow out heavy hip (medium pressure) — continue downward (reducing pressure) to form leg, as shown. With a small cut point (#3), black icing, add a bouncing line (light pressure) for mane, a series of flared lines for tail, and a small shell at end of each leg for hooves. With a fine cut point (#3), white, (light pressure) pull out tiny lines for "feathering" over hooves; insert tube at top of head and (moving downward to nose) blow out white blaze. With a fine cut point (#3), gray, pull two tiny lines upward for ears — add arched lines over eyes and over each nostril — insert tube under ear and (light pressure) blow out a downward-curving, tapering line that finishes as an open mouth. Add two, tiny white eyeballs with black piping jelly pupils. Black piping jelly is also used in nostrils and to outline mouth.

Santa's Reindeer

SLEIGH . . . With a medium cut point (#7) and red icing, outline shape of sleigh — fill in and smooth off with a small palette knife. Try to get top of sleigh (where Santa sits) built up a little thicker than bottom (where runners are). With a fine cut point (#3), gold icing, outline sleigh — add runner on far side and over it pipe runner on near side, as shown.

SANTA . . . Using same red tube, as for sleigh, pipe a tapering line upward (heavy pressure) for body. Leave room for the face and add a tapering line (medium pressure) for hat. Insert tube at shoulders and (medium pressure) pipe two bent lines for arms. (Note: Be sure to bend the near arm over itself to create illusion of holding bag.) **BAG** . . . Use a medium cut point (#7), light yellow icing — with medium pressure, pipe an irregular ball for bulk of bag — continue (tapering line) over Santa's shoulder, piping downward past end of bent over arm. **FACE** . . . With a fine cut point (#3), pink, pipe an oval for face; add two balls for cheeks and a smaller ball, above them, for nose.

TRIM . . . Use a fine cut point (#2), white icing — add fur trim to Santa's outfit (slight "bouncing" motion); pull hair and beard downward; add eyebrows and handlebar mustache. Use fine cut points for blue piping jelly eyes, black icing belt, and gold icing buckle. Use a #3 round tube (red) for mittens; pipe a short, heavy line outward from each sleeve and (light pressure) add a thumb to mitten on "waving hand."

REINDEER . . . Reindeer grouped in this manner will fit easily on a ½ sheet cake. As repetition sharpens skill, and increases speed, the same pressure and movements are used for the heads, necks, bodies and tails of all the reindeer. The leg positions are changed to give them individuality. With a medium cut point (#7), tan icing (medium pressure), pipe a downward curving line for the neck — pause — increase pressure — and pipe a longer, hot-dog-shaped line for body. Return to start of neck and add a tapering line for head. With lighter pressure, add a small, tapering line for ear and pull out a "flip" for tail. When adding legs, start with the two on far side; insert tube into edge of

body and (light pressure) pull out long thin legs in desired positions. When adding the two legs on the near side, insert tube into body at shoulder — blow out shoulder — then (light pressure) continue downward in position desired; insert tube into body at rump — blow out rump — and (light pressure) continue downward in desired position. (Note: Near side legs may cross over, or even conceal, far side legs.) **REINDEER HEAD TRIM** . . . With a fine cut point (#3), tan icing, add a small, curving line over eye and around nostril; insert tube under ear and (medium pressure) blow out downward curv-in line for jaw — decrease pressure — continue downward, ending in closed mouth. Add eye, nostril, mouth line, and split hooves with a fine cut point (#2) and black icing. Using a fine cut point (#3), brown icing, light pressure, pipe a basic line (upward) for each antler, then add prongs to basic line. **HARNESS** . . . With a fine cut point (#3), red icing and light pressure, pipe harness lines from lead reindeer back to sleigh; with same size tube (gold) add sleigh bells to each reindeer's harness.

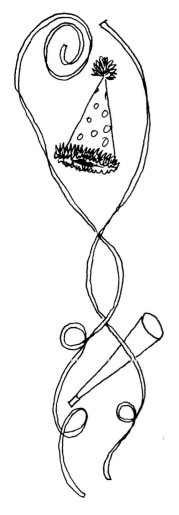

Pink Elephants Everywhere!

A great cake for the "New Year" or year-round parties — pink elephants romp playfully over this yellow iced, ¼ sheet cake. A plastic champagne glass is used for extra height and as a prop, so the elephants may be put in unusual positions, e.g., crawling under the stem, curled up in the bowl or leaning against the base. Confetti is added for a festive touch.

PINK ELEPHANT IN GLASS . . .
Pink elephants piped into plastic champagne glasses make unusual, indi-vidualized place markers or party favors. For ease of production, remove the base of the glass and push the stem into a block of styrofoam; this will hold the glass steady and prevent it from tipping over when you pipe in the elephant. Plastic champagne glasses have a hollow stem; to prevent the icing from going down this stem, pipe the elephant around it or cover the hole with a piece of clear, cellophane tape and pipe the elephant over it.

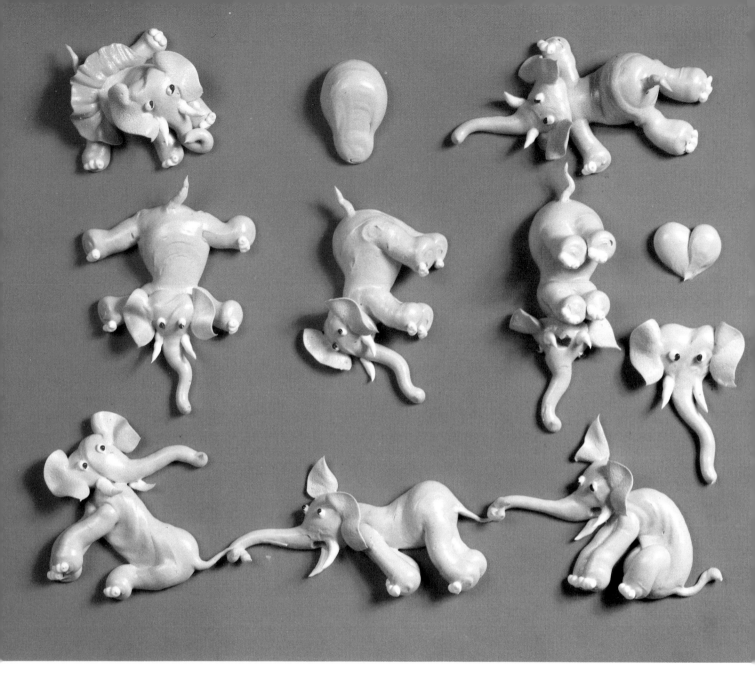

ELEPHANTS . . . As the elephants are large figures, use a large bag of icing (12x18 rectangular parchment) and a #10 round tube with pink icing. **BODY** . . . To make an elephant, start with a large, pear-shaped body (top row center); hold the tube vertically, and (heavy pressure) form a large, round ball — with decreasing pressure, pipe forward to a blunt end. Accentuate the rear end (get it higher) by lifting the tube as you form the ball. The same pear-shaped body is used for all three elephants in the second row — only the leg and head positions are different. The position of the body may be varied in several ways (1) by slightly bending the pear shape (third row); (2) by lifting the front part of the body up off the cake and supporting it with the front legs (top row, left); (3) by lifting rear of body up off the cake and supporting it with the rear legs (top row, right). This last type is used for the elephant crawling under stem of champagne glass on cake. **LEGS** . . . All legs are made in same basic manner — insert tube into body and pull out leg — stop pressure — push back and circle to form a blunt end. By changing the positions of the legs you will have an elephant on his stomach, side, or back. **HEAD** . . . The head is a heavy heart-shape (two over-lapping shells) that is continued downward (light pressure) to form the trunk. **TRIM** . . . Tails are made with a fine cut point (#3), pink icing; insert into rear and pull out. For ears, use a #104 rose tube (wide edge against head); with light pressure, pull ear down — or up — whichever you find easier. The toenails, tusks, and eye-balls are made with a fine cut point (#3), white icing. Three little "bounces" on the edge of each foot form the toenails; tusks are pulled out from each side of the trunk. Pipe a white dot for each eye; add a smaller dot of pink piping jelly for pupils. The positioning of the pupil (in center or near edge of eye) will give a different "look" to each elephant. The elephant's mouth is beneath his trunk; on those whose mouths will show, use a fine point palette knife to scoop it open. To create a "girl" elephant, add a ruffled skirt using a #104 rose tube (blunt edge against body), very light pressure and a slight back-and-forth motion.

How many times have you sat in an overstuffed chair to read a paper, hold a child, watch TV or just relax and take a snooze? All these "moments of life" may be duplicated (upright) on top of a cake.

A) . . . Cut out a strip of white cake (approximately 2½"x5½") and trim a one inch piece off this for seat of chair. Stand tall piece up for back of chair (if making on cake top, run a straw down through it—into cake— to prevent its falling over). Trim a tapered strip from front side of chair's back, so figure will lean back. Add chair arms using small pieces of cake.

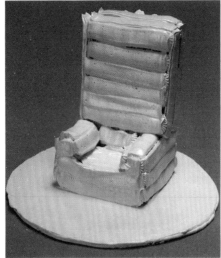

B) . . . Fasten all pieces together with icing, then rough ice chair, in tan, using a #48 tube (smooth side out).

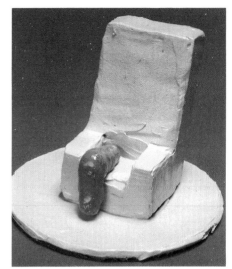

C) . . . Smooth icing with a small spatula or artist's palette knife. For leg, use a medium cut point (#7), brown icing (medium pressure), and pull a line from back of seat to front of seat, bending at knee and continuing downward to rug.

D) . . . Add second leg as in "C". For body, use a medium cut point (#7), green; with tube pointing at back of chair, start at top of legs and run body up back of chair (medium pressure) finishing with shoulders. For heavier stomach, squeeze harder in stomach area. To broaden shoulders, move tube back-and-forth while gently squeezing.

E) . . . For sleeves, insert tube at shoulder and (lighter pressure) come down side of chest — pause at the elbow — change direction — pull sleeve forward, resting it on arm of chair. Repeat for other side. Scoop out hole where neck will go; with light pressure, add horseshoe-shaped ring around hole, for open collar.

F) . . . Add shoes or slippers using a fine cut point (#3) — pull out from bottom of pants (light pressure). Hands are made with a #2 tube (flesh colored icing) — make a light line across ends of sleeves, for palm, then pull out four fingers and thumb (starting with little finger). Head is made like Queen's head, page 25.

Relax, you've earned it...

MAN IN CHAIR CAKE

Iced in a rich, dark-chocolate butter-cream (a favorite with most men), this ¼ sheet cake requires very little extra decoration—everything is concentrated on the figure and its immediate surroundings. A great cake for Father's Day, retirement or for someone planning to enjoy his vacation "relaxing" at home.

The rug is very easily made and like "straw", in the Pig Cake, it creates the illusion of a larger decorated area. Use a medium star tube #18, orange icing, and with a slight back-and-forth motion pipe a large oval — filling in from outside to center. The man in the chair can be made as shown in the step-by-step pictures or a footstool may be added, using a small square of cake or a marshmallow. If using a foot-stool, chair should be placed a little farther back on the rug. After placing chair on rug, be sure to run a straw down — through back of chair — and well into the base cake. Cut off any excess straw extending above back of

chair. Ice chair and footstool (if used) and add figure. Figure using footstool has been altered by placing legs on top of footstool and adding a news-paper (piped upward from lap) with a #104 rose tube. Pull arms towards the newspaper and pipe the fingers around it; "fake" the newsprint with a fine point of black. Socks are heavy lines pulled upward from pant legs. Shoes on rug are made with a fine point of black icing. **CAT** . . . The cat is very similar to the little black bear made previously — a heavy shell, tapering to the "ball" head, and a tiny nose. Pull out long, thin lines for front legs and tail; blow out the hip (from inside) and pull out a thin line for the hind leg. Add tiny pointed ears. Pipe yellow dots for eyes and add pupils and nose accent. **DOG** . . . The dog is made in same basic manner as Ram on page 19. **TRIM** . . . An orange strip is run around bottom of cake with a #104 rose tube; a #18 star tube is used for upward shells, at cor-ners of cake, and for yellow trim on rug.

LADY IN CHAIR

Same old chair — different figure. This time we have a lady in bathrobe, holding a baby. The figure is made in the same basic way as that of the man. Use a medium cut point (#7), yellow icing, medium pressure — start at waist and continue downward to feet, ending in a swirl for bottom of robe. Start at waist and continue up-ward to shoulders; pull out arms, ending with a slight swirl for loose sleeves. Add heavy lapels coming downward. With a fine point palette knife, scoop out a hole in collar and in ends of sleeves. (Note: If adding baby, pipe in "baby bundle" before adding second arm.) Add hands, slip-pers, and head.

Queen for The Day

QUEEN CAKE . . . "Let them eat Cake" — the chair becomes a throne for a little "princess" or for Mother, "Queen of the family". To accomplish this transformation — cut top of chair to a point, ice throne in dark brown (#48 basket tube, smooth side up), smooth off, and using a #15 star tube, outline throne. Pipe royal robe in same manner as bathrobe on lady in chair; except — pipe the collar up in an arch, make sleeve ends fuller, and swirl bottom of robe around base of throne. The swirling part need not be smooth as a few flowing lines will enhance its natural appearance. Trim robe as shown using a medium cut point (#5), white icing, and a fine cut point (#2), black icing. Scoop out hole at neck and at ends of sleeves; add hands, neck and head. **NECK & HEAD** . . . Use flesh colored icing and a medium cut point (#5). A) . . . Starting at bottom of "scooped" hole in collar, go upward for the neck (light pressure) — increase pressure, and form an oval for head. Blow out forehead by inserting tube at top of oval, on one side, and (gentle pressure) moving across to other side. B) . . . Drop down (leave space for the eye) and insert tube at cheek — squeeze a small ball, tapering down to the chin. C) . . . Blow out other cheek, taper downward, and finish with tiny ball for chin. D) . . . Insert tube in center of forehead and with very light pressure draw line downward for nose, ending with a small loop. Pipe two, curved lines for ears. Use a very fine cut point (#2), brown icing, for eyebrows and flowing lines of the hair. With tiny points of piping jelly, add the eyes and mouth. **CROWN** . . . Pipe a flat, red ball on top of head; over this, pipe three, arched, vertical lines (one at each side and one at center of ball) in yellowish-gold; add a curved, gold line at bottom of ball (going from side to side) and a curved white line beneath it — these two "bottom" lines form base of crown.

The chain, gems, and pearls or crown are made with very fine points. **HANDS** . . . Use a very fine cut point (#2) and flesh colored icing — insert tube into scooped out slit in sleeve — squeeze a small ball for the palm, and with very light pressure, pull out the little finger; add other fingers and thumb, working your way upward. Push back at tips of each finger for a blunt end. Repeat for other hand. Add rings and fingernails. (Note: Prevent the queen from "losing her head" by making head and crown tightly against arching collar and throne; as there is no back to head or crown, the long hair also serves as support.) If a larger cake is desired, the red carpet may be continued down a series of one layer cakes (each cake increasing in size) creating a stairway effect.

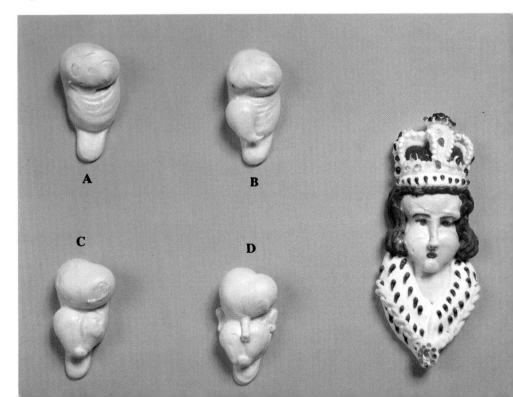

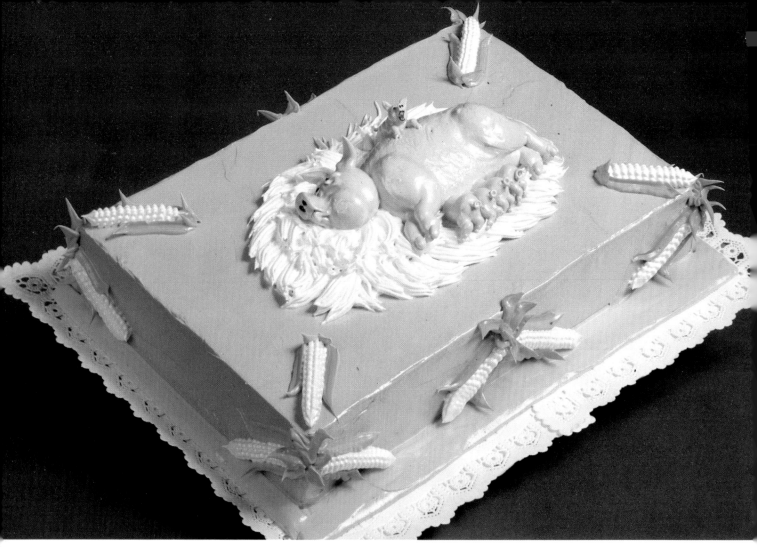

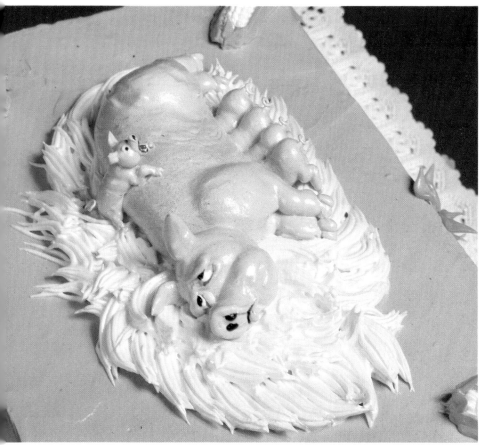

Mother Love...

This ¼ sheet cake, with mamma pig and her piglets, is iced in light tan or mocha. The yellow straw bed is made with a #133/233 tube, using short strokes and light pressure. In addition to providing a bed for the pig family, it also gives the illusion of a larger decorated area.

MAMMA PIG . . . The large body is made in one continuous line, using a #10 round tube and pink icing. Pipe slowly with heavy pressure; apply more pressure in center of body to arch back and stomach. If you cannot squeeze this hard, make body in two arched lines (back and stomach) fill in and smooth off. Legs resting on the cake are made first. Insert tube at front of body and with light pressure pull the short front leg down, forward, and down. Insert tube at rear of body (medium pressure) pull down and to the rear; reduce pressure rapidly and continue downward. For remaining front leg, insert tube half way up body

and with medium pressure blow out the shoulder; reduce pressure, pull downward, forward, and downward again. For rear leg, insert tube half way up body and with heavy pressure build up the "ham"; reduce pressure and pull towards the rear and downward finishing the leg. For the head, tube should point straight at the front of pig (at a low angle). Pipe a round "head" ball, reduce pressure, and pull the snout out and upward; stop pressure, push back and circle to form blunt end on snout. Insert tube on side of head and blow out jowl. Add protruding line for lower lip using small cut point (#3).

PIGLETS . . . With medium cut point (#7) and medium pressure, pull four short lines out (upward) from Mamma's tummy for bodies of piglets. To make "lost" little pig, draw a line up mother's back (#7), medium pressure), adding a ball for the head. Pipe two hind legs for each piglet with

a fine cut point (#3); insert tube at rump and with light pressure come down and towards you, then, down to the straw. If legs are too long add more straw. Only the lost piglet gets two front legs made by inserting tube under piglets head and pulling lines forward onto Mamma's body. Pull out tiny snout and with almost no pressure, pull tube down and out to form lower jaw. If necessary, a toothpick may be used to open the mouth more.

TRIM . . . With a fine cut point (#3), return to mother pig's head and add a ring around the snout, bags under the eyes, sagging lines over the eyes, and a line for the lower lip. With same tube, pipe hooves on mother and lost piglet — two short lines at end of each leg to form a split hoof. Everybody gets a tail . . . insert #3 tube into rump and with light pressure pull out and form a loose open circle. Piglets ears are made using tiny leaf cut point; use larger leaf cut or #67 for mother's ears. A fine cut point of

black piping jelly is used for piglets eyes, nostrils and to outline open mouth; draw a line for mother's mouth and two dots for nostrils. For eyes, pipe two small balls of white icing (underneath sagging lines) and add a dot of black piping jelly at the upper part of each ball . . . in that patient, loving, long suffering look that only motherhood knows.

CORN . . . Use same tube as one used for straw #133/233; hold tube at a low angle and with very light pressure and slight up and down movement, bounce tube the length of the ear of corn (corn figures 1 & 2). An alternate way (Fig. 3 & 4), is to pipe a medium heavy line for the base of corn, then, with fine cut point (#3) hold tube at a low angle (light pressure) and "bounce" kernels on — one row at a time. A darker green, medium cut leaf (#67) is used to pull shucks around the corn.

Bottom border is made with a #48 tube (flat side up).

Extra, Extra Large

OSTRICH ON EGG CAKE

Basically, both of these birds are made the same way — pipe a big, egg-shaped body and insert a plastic straw into the large end; cut straw off (at proper height) to form neck. Only the colors and method of trim are different.

OSTRICH . . . This is a good presentation cake for a job well done or a giant "boo-boo"; an inscription might read "Congratulations, you have accomplished the impossible" or "When you 'lay an egg' you really do it!" A Lady Mary board, with the plastic pin in the bottom, was used to add color and to steady the egg. The cake-egg halves were baked in the large (7") Nordic Ware mold, then joined together with buttercream icing. (Egg may be iced in buttercream or boiled icing.) The easiest way to ice this odd-shaped cake is with a large basket tube (#47st) smooth side out. Pipe on icing — if boiled icing, smooth with a palette knife—for buttercream, use a soft, flat, artist's brush dipped in hot water. After cake is iced, pipe a ring of icing around bottom of egg (on doily) as an additional aid to the egg's stability. The yellow straw (#133/233 tube, short strokes, light pressure) will conceal the ring. With dark gray icing and a #10 round tube, pipe an egg-shaped body on top of the cake-egg; insert a plastic straw, at front part of body, for the neck. If using buttercream, wrap the straw with masking tape to keep the icing from slipping. Use a #10 round tube, pink icing — insert tube on side of body and pull out a heavy, short, tapering line for the thigh. Repeat on opposite side. With gentle pressure, go up back of straw (bottom to top) — repeat on front side, but at top of straw, let icing roll over straw to form a ball for the head. Cover seams on sides of neck by running the #10 tube (very light pressure) up each side of neck. A medium cut point (#7), white icing, is used for the two, large, white eyeballs. Use a medium leaf cut (#67), white icing, to pull the wings out on each side; start at the bottom and work upward. Tail feathers are pulled upward, for additional height

they may be supported by a small candle. The arched "surprised" line over the eyes is done with a fine cut point (#3), pink icing. Use a medium cut point (#7) and yellow icing for the

legs and feet, and a fine leaf cut (#67) for the bill. Place the black "pupil" dot near the bottom of the white eyeball for that astonished look . . . "What Have I Done?!?"

Are You Ready...

BABY BIRD IN NEST . . . "The surprise of my life — I'm supposed to WHAT? ? ?" This cake could be used for a young person leaving home for the first time, someone starting a new job or any occasion where a person must tackle something new. Use a simple, stacked 8", 6" — the eight inch iced pale blue. With a medium cut point (#7) and dark brown, pipe branches on the blue-iced cake, as shown in picture. The six inch cake is iced in a straw color The nest effect is made by covering the sides and top with short back-and-forth strokes using a medium cut point (#7). As the bird will be in the middle of the nest, less build-up is required there. Body, neck, and head are same as ostrich, only done in pink For the legs, use a #10 round tube; come out from body (for thigh), bend forward, and taper off for drumstick. Add lower part of leg, and a foot (in orange) with a medium cut point (#7). For tail, insert medium cut point (#7), pink icing, and pull up a tapering point. Insert tube at front of body (both sides) and pull out wings — three sections for each wing — short, straight lines, with the last one tapering to a point. The eyes, bill and facial expression are also the same as for ostrich. Tiny blue "flight-feathers" are made using a fine cut leaf (#65) and short strokes. Cut a small piece of cardboard, fold in middle, and ice front side brown; write inscription on brown side and insert card between wings.

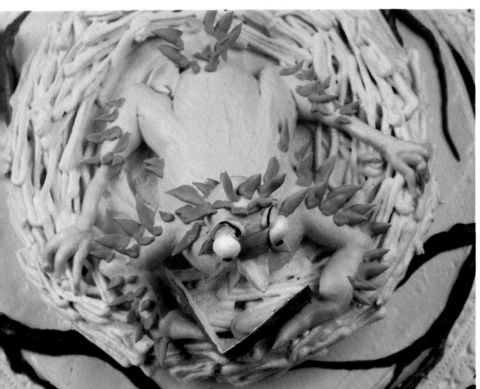

29

Not a Hair Out of Place

CAT CAKE

This cake is a good example of using your family pet to create a fun cake. Rascal (our lovable little character) is depicted here in his "tummy cleaning" pose, which many cat fanciers will quickly recognize.

An eight inch, one layer cake was used merely to give you some idea of the figure's size. Pink icing was selected for contrast. Notice, the body, neck and head -– the bulk of the cat — are all one continuous, heavy, tapering line. Use a large round tube (#10) and white icing for the body. Hold tube in a vertical position a little off the cake; squeeze a heavy round ball (heavy pressure) and continue forward (heavy pressure) forming the body; lift tube, decrease pressure and pull the neck upward and toward you. Stop, and with light pressure form a small round ball for the head. The hind leg is made in three sections using a medium cut point (#7) and white icing. Insert tube into side (rear) of "body" ball and (medium pressure) come out in a tapering line curving downward; pause, use light pressure and continue with a short straight line; pause, and finish the leg with a slightly bent line forming a paw at the end. Add second hind leg in same manner. Insert same

tube between legs and pull tail out to desired length. Insert tube into body on side where neck begins to lift upward; pull out (light pressure) a straight line for front leg, ending with a very slight round ball for the paw. Repeat for other front leg. Insert very fine cut point (#2) into each paw and make three continuous rolling circles for toes. Make pink tummy with a medium cut point (#7). Insert tube into body at chest area and with very light pressure (back and forth motion) work your way down length of tummy. Facial features are added using a very slight pressure and a fine cut point (#3), white. Insert tube into top front of the "head" ball on body of cat; with slight pressure, build out a tapering line over each eye — moving from edge to center. Drop down to center of ball, insert tube, and with light pressure pull out a short blunt line for the nose. With a fine cut leaf point (#65) pull up two small ears (set well back on the head). Use a very fine cut point (#2) pink, add a little heart shape on the end of the nose and an upside down "Y" for the mouth. Pull out a tiny, pink tongue in a licking position. Using the same tube, fill in the ears with pink. For the eyes, use a fine cut point (#2) and yellow piping jelly. With the tip of the tube, scoop out two upward-slanting, tapering lines; fill lines with yellow piping jelly and add a black dot for each pupil.

Super-Clown

Perhaps you know someone who is "always the clown" or maybe you just need a "fun" cake for a special party. Why not try this "super clown" that covers the entire cake top. His little, pink friend is an added attraction.

Ice a ¼ sheet cake in warm yellow. For the body, use a #47st basket tube (smooth side up). With a large bag of blue icing and heavy pressure, pipe a big heart shape for the seat of the clown's pants. Do not end heart shape in a point, but continue your pressure and pull the body forward, ending at the shoulders. Insert tube at shoulders and (medium pressure) pull out each arm. Insert tube into rump and (medium pressure) pull out the legs (Note: The arms and legs have blunt ends so the hands and shoes may be more easily attached). Scoop out a hole where the head will go (for better support of the head). With a #104 rose tube (wide edge against body), orange icing and using a "bouncing" motion (light pressure), add ruffles to arms, legs and neck. Using a medium cut point (#7 round) and brown icing, pull out a heavy line for each shoe (heel to toe); add a very light outline around bottom of each shoe for the sole. Use a medium cut point (#7), in white, for the hands. For right hand start against ruffle, make a small line upward for the palm, then, pull out a short curved line for the bottom finger. Repeat for three remaining fingers — one on top of the other. The thumb (fifth line) is pulled out from the upper inside part of the hand. Repeat for left hand, but curl the fingers and thumb, as they will be holding straw containing the umbrella. To add head . . . start in hole (at neck) and pipe a large oval upward, tilting back toward body. Blow out cheeks on each side, pulling downward and ending in a ball for the chin. Blow out the forehead; add a smile line in white (giving the mouth more buildup); and pipe two curved lines for the ears. Cut a small point (#3), use red icing and pipe two small balls for pom-poms on the seat of his pants. Pipe a large ball for the nose. Cut a fine point (#3) use brown icing, add arched eyebrows and pull out the hair. (Hair may be used as additional support for the head.) Eyes, mouth and tirm on face are done with fine points of piping jelly. **PIGGY** . . . Piggy is made with a medium cut point #7 and pink icing. Using heavy pressure, pipe an oval for the body. With light pressure, insert tube into body and pull out two front legs. Insert at rear, blow up the "ham" (from the inside), come out heavy and fade out quickly, while bending the leg as shown in picture. Pipe a round ball for the head; insert tube and blow out both jowls. Insert tube between and slightly above jowls and pull out a short (upward) line; stop pressure, push back and circle for blunt pig snout. Use a fine cut point (#3), add curly tail, little split hooves, accent lines over eyes and ring around end of snout. Cut a fine leaf point (#65) to use for the ears. Black piping jelly dots are added for eyes and nostrils.

The #104 rose (orange) used for the ruffles is run around the bottom of cake for the border; thin lines of red and blue are added for accent. Place a cocktail straw in the clown's curled hand (pushing straw well into cake) and insert a paper umbrella into straw. This will add height to the decoration. For a finishing touch, sprinkle cake with candy confetti.

Congratulations on your Promotion!

SCARECROW CAKE

For the office party, the farmer (weekend or full time) or your own special occasion, try this happy scarecrow.

Ice a ¼ sheet cake in light blue; with a medium cut point (#7), blue icing, start in middle of cake (use medium pressure) and draw one leg downward, stopping in a blunt end. Return to starting point (insert tube at top of first leg) and repeat procedure for second leg. Using a medium cut point (#7), orange, start at top of pants and draw a line upward (medium pressure) for the shirt; add two curved lines for the collar (light pressure). For jacket, use a medium cut point (#7), brown icing, and medium pressure — on side of shirt, draw a line upward to the shoulder; stop at the shoulder, lighten pressure, and draw a line outward for the arm, finishing in a blunt end. Repeat for other side. On each side of jacket front draw a tapering, downward line (light pressure) for the lapels. (Notice how we have used three lines to create the width of the body, as opposed to one heavy line used in some other figures, such as the clown.) Pipe an oval shape for the head (above collar) using a medium cut point (#7) and an off

white color. With a fine cut point (#3), dark brown icing, pipe a short line outward from each pant leg for the shoes; outline the bottom of each shoe (very fine line) for the sole. Using same tube, make a double-humped line on the top of scarecrow's head for crown of hat. Cut off the paper tube above ½ inch back) — slip a #104 rose tube over the outside — hold tube in place, and (blunt end down) draw a line across head for brim of hat. With a fine cut point (#2), add a small blue line at end of sleeves; from this line, pull the dangling fingers downward, using a fine cut point (#3), white icing, and very light pressure. Very fine points (red & black) are used for the features on face. With very

fine cut point (yellow) pull out clusters of fine lines for leaking stuffing. Use a medium cut point (#7), black icing, (light pressure) and pipe crows upward from scarecrow's arms; to form each crow, pipe a short line (upward) ending in a "ball" head; add a small, tapering line (downward) for the wing, fine yellow points (outward) for the bill, yellow dots for eyes, and tiny lines for the feet. Add a smear of brown icing for the dirt below the scarecrow's feet and a line of gray icing (piped downward from pants to the dirt) for the pole that supports him. For the sprouting crop, green grass-type tufts are piped with a fine cut leaf (#65). A #18 star tube (yellow) is used for the border.